Rabbit's BIG Idea

Elise De Silva

EDS PUBLISHING

ISBN: 978-0-473-33356-0

First published in 2015 by EDS Publishing.

Text and illustrations copyright © Elise De Silva 2015

Design, Typesetting and Cover Design copyright © 2015 EDS Publishing

The author/illustrator asserts the moral right to be identified as the author/illustrator of the work.
Thank you Naomi for pencil sketches on pages 6 and 7.
Thank you Rebekah for text on pages 6, 7 and 9.

www.edspublishing.com

One evening, while the moon played dot-to-dot with the stars, Rabbit was woken up by something strange...

It was an idea!

The idea started out quiet as a whisper,
but by the time the moon had peeked
in at the window,

tiptoed below the
horizon,

and sent the sun to say,
'Hello,' Rabbit's idea
had become...

a Big Idea!

Fix the Park
Need to:
. Fix swing
. Plant flowers
. Plant trees
. Clean up rubbich
. Get helpers
SEEDS
SEEDS

Rabbit was very proud.

Rabbit wanted his Big Idea to happen more than he'd
ever wanted anything. He told his family about his
Big Idea.
They had their doubts.

'You're very small for such a Big Idea, Rabbit,' said Brother.

'Why, yes,' said Sister. 'And Big Ideas can lead to big disappointments.'

'True. And big disappointments can be really disappointing,' said Cousin.

So Rabbit locked his idea away.

He kept it hidden for a very long time, but Rabbit could not forget it. He missed his Big Idea. He still wanted it to happen more than he'd ever wanted anything.

So one day, Rabbit unlocked his idea and tried again. He worked very hard. His idea grew and grew until it became a Big Idea once more.

He was so proud.

He took his Big Idea to the Right People, people that
dealt with big ideas every day. They looked at it and
they studied it. They *hmmmed* and they *hahhed.*
They calculated this and they calculated that.
Finally, the Right People said,
'Sorry, not interested.'

They didn't like Rabbit's Big Idea. They said no-one else would like it either. They said it was the Wrong Idea.

Poor Rabbit.

A bird saw Rabbit crying and flew down next to him. 'Why are you crying, little rabbit?' she asked.

And Rabbit said,

Bird smiled at Rabbit. 'No, it's not a Bad Idea,' she said, 'It's a *New* Idea. A lot of people are scared of New Ideas.'
'They are?' said Rabbit.
'Oh, yes,' said Bird.
'Then what should I do?' asked Rabbit.

'Well, with any New Idea you have to be brave. You also have to persevere. But most of all, you have to *believe*.'

So Rabbit went home, took a deep breath, and worked on his Big Idea once more.

To Do List
1
2
3
4
5
6
7
8
9

When he worried about what his family might think, he was brave and carried on.

When he imagined the Right People saying *sorry, not interested* again, he persevered and refused to give up.

And when days and weeks and months passed, and he
thought his Big Idea might never happen, he *believed*.

Until, one day...

PAPER
GLASS

Rabbit was so proud.

What is your Big Idea?